THE LAST SECOND GUIDE TO:
Quickly Writing A Research Paper or Report

Deadline beating strategies for getting a paper written at the last minute

Jesse Horn

FyreFly LLC
PRESS

Fyrefly Press Copyright 2016

Contents

Introduction (*Shortcut*)

One of the most challenging parts about being a student in our modern world is our inability to keep up with what is expected of us. To do this often times you may find yourself fighting against the clock in order to get your work done and all of the other elements that are required of you. If you are like the countless others out there who have found themselves up against a deadline you need help and the kind of help that needs to come fast.

If this is not the first time you have been faced with a deadline like this, it is likely not going to be your last either. There are many online options out there to help you get a paper quick, for the right price, but how do you know what you are getting and this option doesn't quite fix the ultimate problem. As previously stated you are going to need to write research papers and reports again in the future. Like the Chinese proverb says "Give a man a fish and you feed him for a day. Teach a man to fish and you feed him for a lifetime". You need to do this on your own, but you need the skills to do this.

This guide is designed to be a good quick resource for you to effectively write a research paper or report that will get you a good grade fast. This will still take some time on your part, however by using this guide you can write an original multipage report in just a couple of hours. In order for you to do this you need to understand some basic things.

- First of all you need to eliminate distractions. Having music, television, or other people in the room with you can be nice, but if you are in a hurry you need to concentrate and these things can be a distraction.

- Secondly, make sure you have something to drink and snack on. Having to stop and get these items while in the process of writing can also become a distraction and lead you to wasting valuable time.

- Third, you will need an internet connection and a computer. The method for doing this quickly will require access to the internet.

In addition to these items there is a few others you should also be aware of.

First disclaimer: This is a method designed to get you quick and effective results. This is by no means a substitute for traditional research, writing and teaching. It should honestly not be used unless you are out of other options, although some of the techniques are still useful in conjunction with traditional methods. This is also no guarantee for success. If followed correctly there is a high probability that you will be able to get a good grade in time for your deadline. However, this is subjective and requires your good effort. As a result it will only be as good as what you are able to put in to it.

Second disclaimer: The methods used to accomplish this goal are tactics used by web content creators and news paper reporters who need to get results fast. If you are not aware web content creators are writers who get paid a very little amount of money to write a vast number of pages of content for website owners. In order for them to be successful they need to create a large volume of good quality work in a very short amount of time. This means that they will often get an assignment for a keyword topic, and have to research it, write it, and have it resubmitted (often times in multiple unique versions) within 30 minutes to an hour or their rate of pay gets smaller. The average title will need to be 500 to 1000 words long. In order to accomplish this often times the writer will create the first document, and then have to "spin" the additional documents.

Spinning is the practice of taking an original text and rewriting it so that it can pass any plagiarism test. This guide will teach you some quick methods of accomplishing this.

To use this guide note that there are eight sections. Each one is broken down with explanations on how to accomplish certain goals. Throughout the text there are

(*Shortcut*) tabs that will help you get to the heart of what you need to do (for those in a REAL hurry) however it is recommended that you read the entire text to get the full benefit. An average reader and writer should be able to get through this text, do the needed research and write the full report, depending upon length needed, within 3 1/2 hours.

Shortcut

Don't expect magic. However if you put effort in you will get results out. The goal is to stay focused and use the techniques described here.

TiP : **When writing a research paper or report quickly it is critical that you:** *Keep your mind open to change and don't get stuck on one idea. If things are moving in a different direction you need to be willing to change them up for the sake of quick completion*

BACK

Getting set up and started (*Shortcut*)

In order to get a research paper or report done quickly it is important that you set up your mind properly regarding how to look at what you are needing to do. First of all it is about putting a bunch of ideas together and making it all work in a way that makes sense to the teacher. Think about it like playing connect the dots, only you are the one both making the picture and connecting them in the end. When researching you will be putting the dots of the picture together, then when you write the paper you will be connecting the dots.

Determine your needs

This means that you will need to know what is expected of you for the paper. This includes knowing what sources you need to have. Does your teacher require that you have only so many internet based sources? Do you have to have book or paper sources? How long does your paper need to be? What format does it need to be written in, APA, MLA or something else? Will you need a work cited page or bibliography page?

This is the framework that you will work around as you are collecting your information. It is important that you understand that to do this quickly you will need to keep a balance between what your research topic is, and the information you collect, more on this later.

What does it all mean?

Sources:

Don't be worried by the number or type of sources you need to collect for the paper. Many people panic when they realize that they need to come up with a couple of book sources the night before the paper is due and they have no way of getting to the library or other resources. There are ways around this, but you have to be creative (and no you are not going to make something up, I'll show you how to find this information online).

Citations and style:

Style is another element that trips people up and one that is truly not as important as other aspects. You might find yourself getting marked down for a few little mistakes, but the important thing is that you get the paper turned in and in the best condition possible. When it comes to ensuring that you have good citations, both for your *work cited* page and in text citations (if needed) there are some fantastic websites that can do all the work for you. One of the best ones out there is Son of a Citation Machine (citationmachine.net). This is a website that you select the style needed, including the type of material you are using, and it will generate a citation based on the information you give it.

Word Count:

If you have been given a guideline for how many pages you are needed to produce there is a good rule of thumb to follow. A page in word is approximately 500 words long. Therefore you can estimate that if you need to write a two page report, double spaced in size 12 font you will only really need to write 500 words. This is not exact, but a good way to gauge what you need to do.

Picking a topic

To start you will need to pick a topic. This may be something that your teacher has already assigned to you, or you may have a general idea of what needs to be done, and you have to fine tune that to something specific. If at all possible try and choose something that can overlap with a topic you have already studied or interests you. This can be a big help.

When coming up with ideas try and word them in two ways:

- *Topic headings*
- *Sentence already containing idea*

To find a topic to write about try doing a quick search on these two ideas to see what comes up. Try to use Google if it all possible. There are other search engines that may be effective, but if you are in a hurry and need good all inclusive results Google will help you get there faster.

The final results you need to look for after these searches are something that gets not only a lot of hits, but ones that are useful. For example, let's say you need to do a research paper on the question "**Should parents bribe children, and if so, what are appropriate bribes**?" you would first search the topic as stated. Typical results for this search give:

Parents bribing kids for good behavior - Health - **Children's** health ...
www.nbcnews.com/id/...childrens.../parents-buying-kids-good-behavior/ ▾
Apr 16, 2007 – "I'm **sure our parents** would be appalled **if** they knew how much we
bribe our **children**." She **can** see why they might be — **but** she and her ...

Bribing Kids vs. Rewarding **Kids** for Good Behavior: What's the ...
www.empoweringparents.com › ... › Abusive And Violent Behavior ▾
Rewarding **kids** for behaving **appropriately** and not **bribing** them under duress ... **Kids**
can come to expect something extra for simply executing their daily ... The **parent** is
frustrated and embarrassed, **so** she proposes a deal: **If** the **kids** will ...

Pay for Grades: **Should Parents Bribe Kids** in School? - TIME
www.time.com/time/magazine/article/0,9171,1978758,00.html
Apr 8, 2010 – **Should Kids** Be Bribed to Do Well in School? ... **If** he could go a full
month without watching any TV, she would give him $200. ... The Bible repeatedly
commands **children** to heed their **parents** and proposes that disobedient ... **But** all this
time, there has been only one real question, particularly in America's ...

Child Discipline - The Bad News About Using **Bribes**
childcare.about.com › ... › Child Behavior › Behaviors and Discipline ▾
While **bribes** typically do get the desired action in the short-term, **parents** may be ...
But does **bribing** (or "rewarding" a **child**, **if** you want to say it more nicely) truly work?
... Rather, it **should** be something like an outing to the park, playing a favorite ... **If** your
child behaves **appropriately**, you'll then head out to the park for some ...

Train a **Parent**, Spare a **Child** - The New York Times
www.nytimes.com/.../modifying-a-childs-behavior-without-resorting-to-bri...
Jan 11, 2013 – Teaching **parents** an alternative to **bribes** when **children** balk. ...
Motherlode Blog: In Defense of **Child** Bribery (January 11, 2013) ... "If you want
somebody to do something, and **if** you have enough money, you **can** get them do it," he
said. ... **But** with **children**, he pointed out, since you are trying to get them to ...

Bribing Kids for Good Behavior - WebMD
www.webmd.com/**parenting**/features/**bribing-kids**-for-good-behavior ▾
Lots of **parents** do it, **but bribing** your **children can** backfire. WebMD Feature Archive
... "Daddy, what do we get if we're good in the store?" Parenting expert Jim ...

This includes some good links to news reports, parenting sites, and sites related to the
medical world. Changing the wording a little and using Google's auto fill option can also

lead you to results you might have not otherwise found. For this same example you can start typing the question "**Is bribing children...**" and allow Google to start populating results.

is bribing children bad

is bribing children **bad**

does bribing children **work**

About 8,140,000 results (0.41 seconds)

Why It's Not Such a Good Idea to **Bribe Kids** for Good Behavior
www.webmd.com/parenting/features/**bribing-kids**-for-good-behavior ▾
WebMD asked experts and parents about the alternatives to **bribing kids** for good ...
cycle of crying and **bad** behavior, says Elizabeth Pantley, parenting educator ...

The Right Way to **Bribe** Your **Child** - Parenting.com
www.parenting.com/article/the-right-way-to-**bribe**-your-**child** ▾
Bribes that would not only give him a small amount of pleasure, but, perhaps ... Silly games can also inspire good **behavior and divert kids** from **bad** behavior.

Child Discipline - The **Bad** News About Using **Bribes**
childcare.about.com › ... › Child Behavior › Behaviors and Discipline ▾
What parent hasn't **bribed a child** to stay quiet, do something he doesn't want to do, or to try a new food. While **bribes** typically do get the desired action in the ...

Modifying a **Child's** Behavior Without Resorting to **Bribes** – This Life ...
www.nytimes.com/.../modifying-a-**childs**-behavior-without-resorting-to-**bri**... ▾
Jan 11, 2013 – Teaching parents an alternative to **bribes** when **children** balk. ...
Without thinking, I said, "more creative **bribing**." ... So I got it: **bribing** is **bad**.

New Book Suggests **Bribing Kids** Is A **Bad** Parenting Tactic
www.mommyish.com/.../new-book-suggests-**bribing-kids**-is-a-**bad**-paren... ▾
Jan 13, 2013 – New book suggests **bribing kids** is a **bad** parenting tactic and if we can't **bribe** our strong-willed three-year-olds, they suggest we actually ...

The results of this search not only show some alternatives, but a *New York Times* article different than the first results showing a much different direction. The results of these two searches are nearly enough for you to create a well done paper, depending upon your needs.

Some things to consider if you have time

First of all if you do not have time to do extra, or you are in a real hurry, skip this section. However you should consider looking back at it for future reference as this includes some great ideas to add something special to your paper without a lot of extra work. If you have time, or you know you won't have a lot of time in the future but want to be prepared a great way to save you from writing and add something really special is to do email interviews. It is possible that this can be done just a couple of days before the paper is due, but ideally you should try to do this as soon as you know what your topic is.

To do this conduct an internet search on the topic you have been assigned or are choosing and see who the experts in the world are on this already. This can include people who have written academic papers, news articles and books on the subject. Find the authors of these works and locate their contact information. This sounds harder than it is. Many of these people are either affiliated with a news agency or some education foundation. More often than not anyone who has written a book on the subject is also a professor and typically their email address can be found looking on the University website. If it isn't there are other ways to do this. Search their name in various ways. Try using the university website, but rather than putting the www. In front put their name. For John Smith at lazystudentuniversity.com you would try: john.smith@lazystudentuniversity.com, or jsmith@ lazystudentuniversity.com, john@lazystudentuniversity.com. This will sometimes show their email address or a variation of it in a pdf of a school document or other material. If this does not work you can also try contacting the school themselves or the department that they work in.

If you can locate the email address try sending out an email asking really basic questions about the topic. Often times these individuals are anxious to talk about the topic they are already passionate about and this can add a lot to a paper. It can be a great way to impress a teacher, and provide you not only with material that is exclusive to you, but content you don't have to write.

Perspective

Another consideration if you have time is what approach you want the paper to be. Do you want this to be an argumentative research paper, or an analytical research paper. In all reality this is not realistic if you are in a hurry. This requires a good knowledge of the material and great resources, something difficult to do in a short amount of time. I once took the approach this guide is teaching and did an entire Economics class in a weekend.

I guessed through the quizzes quickly made up the grade by writing multiple research papers, all in two days. I pulled off a B+, but unfortunately didn't retain a single thing.

For better explanations of these two approaches see the **glossary** of this guide

Shortcut When it comes to getting things done quick Google is your friend. You need to start with a topic and this is going to be the core of your paper. This is not only because it is what your paper is going to be about, but finding the right one is key. Make sure you do this right at the beginning. By searching the topic you can find out if there is an abundance of information out there already or not. It is fun to do something interesting, but if there isn't a lot of quick info you are going to struggle. Use the search concepts of the *topic* you were given, and use the main idea in a *sentence.* It doesn't have to be a complete sentence, and in fact this can sometimes actually help you. Let Google's auto fill guide you to find more information.

Tip :**When writing a research paper or report quickly it is critical that you:** Just get started! Don't worry about having a catchy beginning or wording things right at the beginning. Jump right in and get going on the body. **START SOMEWHERE!**...you can go back and polish things up (Connect the Dots) later

BACK

How to do quick research (*Shortcut*)

Combined with the idea that your topic is pivotal to the core of your paper, so too is your research. In order to get a paper done quickly you will need to find information about your subject quickly and piece things together. There is a good system that you can follow which will help this along.

Before explaining this method there are a couple of quick things to consider. First of all there is your thesis statement. Any English teacher will direct you to start with this before writing your report as this is what will be the guiding principle behind what you are writing. A thesis is a statement summarizing what your paper is essentially about. Obviously you will only be writing a "Working" thesis statement in this initial first stages, but if this can be helpful for some who need that kind of focus. For the sake of time you will likely only need to you're your original topic or sentence. It is a good idea however to keep a direction in mind as you are compiling information. Be flexible so as to not get stuck trying to write about something you are having difficulty put together, but having a direction can also make the process a little smoother.

The following is some further information regarding a thesis, should your paper require one.. If you are in a hurry **skip** to the next section. It is good to know that a thesis statement is primarily presented as a statement. Basically this is stating something like "blah and blah are correct because of "This", "This" and "This". As a tip it is also best not to weaken your position by using the words "I think", "I believe" or "It is in my opinion". The point of your paper is to prove your thesis is correct. Write a working thesis statement based on the goal of the research paper. A thesis statement summarizes the overall point of a paper by making a claim and then listing points that will be used as evidence to support it. At this point in the process, you should only write a working thesis statement because it may change during the course of your research.

Should your paper be written from an argumentative perspective you will have a thesis statement that states your position on the issue, but also includes key points to what in your research confirms your point.

If you are needing to write a paper with an analytical approach you will need to craft a working thesis in the form of a question. A good example of this might be if you are writing on the book To Kill A Mockingbird. For this you might propose a question such as "what does the role of honor play in this book?".

Websites and appropriate content:

There are many that will tell you should the academic credibility of a source be questioned do not use the source, and they are right…under normal circumstances. If you need results and you need them now you are going to have to take the information from where ever you can get it. Obviously sites that end in .edu or .gov and ones that have a reputation for excellence that has been well established are good choices. When you are in a pintch you are just going to have to make due, the tricky part is making it fly with a teacher.

Wikipedia and biography.com are your friend. So are fan sites and collage sites made by students created for historical figures and events. These are amazing resources that can help get you the bulk of the info you need for just about any site. There are also some free websites that contain student guides to topics and books which have information you can get fairly easily. For public domain work there is www.gutenberg.org which offers thousands of free books both online and in ebook format. The key here is to get the body of the information you need quickly.

Step one:

To start with go back to the search results you previously found while finding a topic. This can be a fantastic starting point. If at all possible try and have your internet browser open only half your screen to three quarters of your screen full, and the remaining space a black document file opened and saved. It is a good idea to save your file so that should something happen and the program crashes you can find the recovery file quickly. There is nothing more frustrating than having to open a million "Document" files trying to find the one you were just working on.

By having two items open in this way you can move quickly from the two programs without having to find each after going to the other.

Step two:

Start skimming through the content on each page and as you find chunks of information that looks like it may contain information that might be useful copy it and paste it into the word document. Label the content according to what the information is about if at all possible. You do not need to completely read the material, just read the first couple of paragraphs and the last couple. This should give you a general idea what it is about and the direction it is heading.

Ask yourself the following questions:

Does this coincide with the topic I am writing about?

Will this content work with other material I have already collected?

Can I change the question I have asked to match what this information is telling me to speed up the writing and research process?

As you go separate this content by hitting enter a few times and after you paste info from a website make sure that you also copy and paste the following other information with it:

- Website URL
- Name of the website
- Name of the content or article you are copying
- Name of the author
- Date it was written
- Current date

This is important information that you will need when putting together citations and having it up front will save you from having to go and try and re-find it later.

Step Three:

Continue this process until you have several pages of content. Try not to grab too much, as you will need to go through this information fairly quickly. It is important that you do not get overwhelmed and depending upon your page count needs a little information can go a long way. On average for a two page report you will want to have about 5 to 10 pages of content to work from.

Getting information from *Book Sources* in a hurry:

As mentioned earlier this can be one of the most challenging and frightening parts of a research paper or report. This primarily happens because students fail to get this information before the deadline is upon them and they end up without a way to get it in time. In addition to this, book information can be difficult to get when you are in a hurry. A great trick to find what you need on a web page or document is using "Ctrl F". This brings up a small search window at the top of your browser that allows you to search the page for particular words or phrases. This can be handy when you are in a hurry, but how can you do this if you are reading a real book. Even skimming a text book or academic material can be a challenge to do fast. The alternative may surprise you.

The reality is your teacher wants you to have this kind of source material in your paper. The end result is that as long as you have this in there you are going to be fine. Make this the last of your concerns as far as real content, although you can find some very useful things when using this information.

To get this information you are going to do another Google search for your topic, however you are going to do it differently this time.

Up in the right hand corner on the black bar running across the page there is a "More" options. Click this.

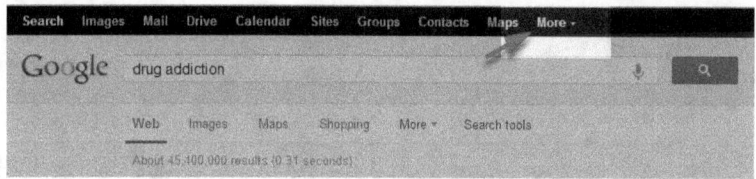

This will give you a drop down and at the bottom is "Even More", click this as well. This will bring you to a screen with a lot of other choices.

Scroll down to the Specialized Search option area and select

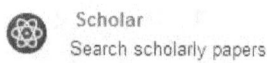

From here conduct your Google search of your topic. For this example we will search the topic "Drug Addiction".

From this result we get at the top of the search several good options such as Molecular mechanisms of drug addiction. This comes from the *Journal of Neuroscience* and is a research paper published in 1992. The *Journal of Neuroscience* is a highly respected publication and comes in both print and web based forms.

drug addiction

Scholar

About 723,000 results (0.03 sec)

Articles

Legal documents

Any time
Since 2013
Since 2012
Since 2009
Custom range...

Sort by relevance
Sort by date

✓ include patents
✓ include citations

✉ Create alert

[CITATION] **Drug addiction** and **drug** abuse
JH Jaffe - The pharmacological basis of ..., 1990 - New York, NY: Pergammon Press
Cited by 1697   Related articles   Cite

Molecular mechanisms of **drug addiction.**
EJ Nestler - The Journal of neuroscience, 1992 - psycnet.apa.org
Abstract 1. Reviews results of research to understand the neurobiological basis of
compulsive **drug** use, focusing on drugs such as opiates and cocaine, since the addictive
mechanisms underlying the actions of these drugs are the best understood. Cellular sites ...
Cited by 642   Related articles   All 5 versions   Cite   More ▾

Neural systems of reinforcement for **drug addiction**: from actions to habits to compulsion
EJ Everitt, TW Robbins - Nature neuroscience, 2005 - nature.com
Abstract **Drug addiction** is increasingly viewed as the endpoint of a series of transitions from
initial **drug** use—when a **drug** is voluntarily taken because it has reinforcing, often hedonic,
effects—through loss of control over this behavior, such that it becomes habitual and ...
Cited by 1263   Related articles   All 15 versions   Cite

Nucleus accumbens shell and core dopamine: differential role in behavior and **addiction.**
GD Chiara - Behavioural brain research, 2002 - psycnet.apa.org
... Chiara, Gaetano Di. Behavioural Brain Research, Vol 137(1-2), Dec 2002, 75-114. doi:
10.1016/S0166-4328(02)00286-3. Abstract. **Drug addiction** can be conceptualized as
a disturbance of behavior motivated by **drug**-conditioned incentives. ...
Cited by 556   Related articles   All 9 versions   Cite

Also note that there is within this "Academic" search filter a "Cite" options.

Molecular mechanisms of **drug addiction**.

EJ Nestler - The Journal of neuroscience, 1992 - psycnet.apa.org
Abstract 1. Reviews results of research to understand the neurobiological basis of
compulsive **drug** use, focusing on drugs such as opiates and cocaine, since the addictive
mechanisms underlying the actions of these drugs are the best understood. Cellular sites ...
Cited by 642   Related articles   All 5 versions   Cite   More ▾

Neural systems of reinforcement for **drug addiction**: from actions to habits to compulsion

BJ Everitt, TW Robbins - Nature neuroscience, 2005 - nature.com
Abstract **Drug addiction** is increasingly viewed as the endpoint of a series of transitions from
initial **drug** use—when a **drug** is voluntarily taken because it has reinforcing, often hedonic

If you click this option you can get various forms of a citation for this content. Save
yourself some time later by going ahead and copying this information and putting it in
your document.

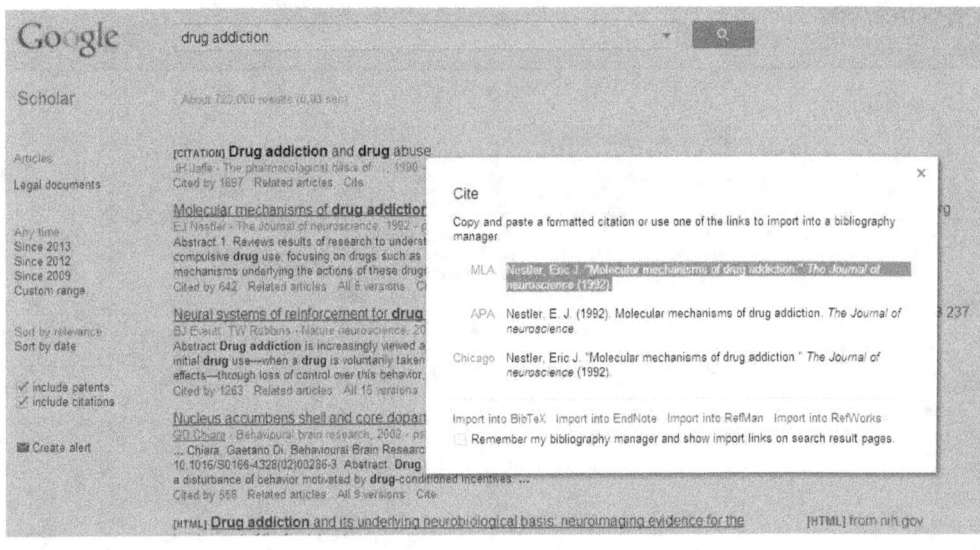

If you click on the link you will find that it leads you to some basic information regarding the paper. This includes, once again, the citation information, as well as an Abstract of the paper. The abstract is honestly all you need to write useful information from a "Book or paper" source.

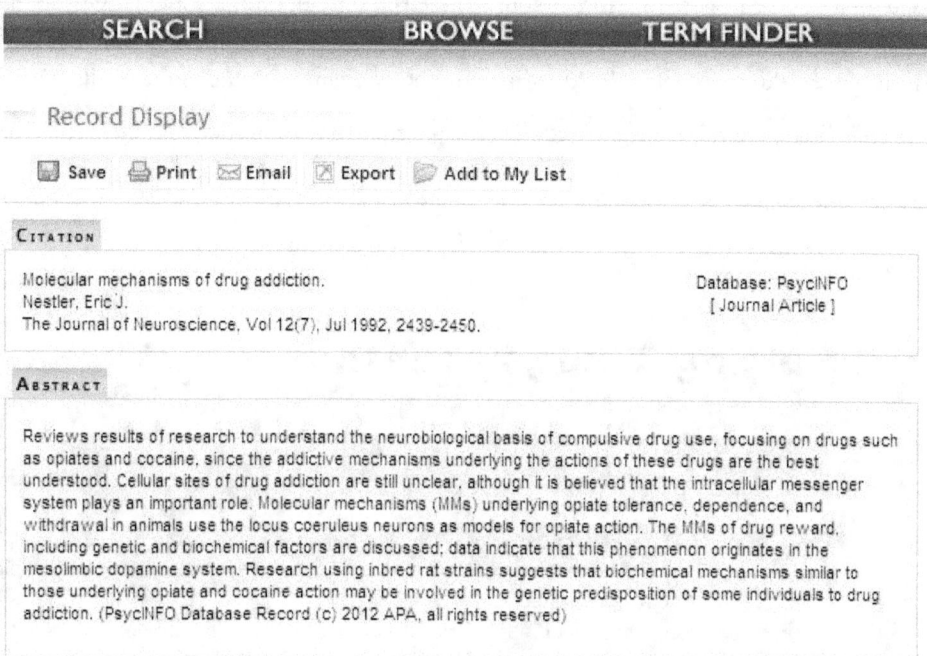

Reviews results of research to understand the neurobiological basis of compulsive drug use, focusing on drugs such as opiates and cocaine, since the addictive mechanisms underlying the actions of these drugs are the best understood. Cellular sites of drug addiction are still unclear, although it is believed that the intracellular messenger system plays an important role. Molecular mechanisms (MMs) underlying opiate tolerance, dependence, and withdrawal in animals use the locus coeruleus neurons as models for opiate action. The MMs of drug reward, including genetic and biochemical factors are discussed; data indicate that this phenomenon originates in the mesolimbic dopamine system. Research using inbred rat strains suggests that biochemical mechanisms similar to those underlying opiate and cocaine action may be involved in the genetic predisposition of some individuals to drug addiction. (PsycINFO Database Record (c) 2012 APA, all rights reserved)

Note the first sentence of *Molecular mechanisms of drug addiction* contains useful information about drug addiction and can add to the overall feel of your paper. If you run into an issue with needing to identify a page number, use page one as this is likely where the Abstract will be located. The likely hood of your teacher calling you out on this is not very big and it is a small thing to be marked off on in the big scheme of things.

TiP : **When writing a research paper or report quickly it is critical that you:** Create citations as you go, don't back track - confusion and having to Re-research will set you back significantly on time

Shortcut When it comes to researching and collecting information quickly it is really effective to search your original topic and gather information that fits together in one document. You can get any kind of source material online, including what will work for book sources and scholarly journals. Don't get to crazy about collecting data, get the bulk from places like news sites, Wikipedia and other websites. You can put it all together later in a way that will be legitimate and original.

BACK

Putting Things together (*Shortcut*)

The "meat" of the paper:

Once you have everything you initially need, which here we will call the "Meat" of the paper you will need to organize it. This will essentially become the paragraphs of the paper where everything is laid out for the reader, all the evidence is presented and you analyze and provide information. If it helps you, particulary if you have a long or involved paper with lots of information, write a brief description of the content. This will serve as a quick way to identify what you are working with. If you do not have a lot of different pieces of content do not waste your time with this. It will take you longer to write these out then it is worth.

First you will need to organize the content into a semi-logical order. This means looking at what you have and placing each one of the pieces in a way that will best fit together in a meaningful way. This also may start out with each being placed in a VERY loosely related way, don't worry about this. The idea here is to just make it all work a little better together for the writing process.

Telling stories

Think about this as telling a story and each one of the pieces that you found are the chapters of that tale. Also keep in mind that at this point you may start to find that your original topic is starting to evolve into something else. As long as this is within the boundaries of what your teacher will be expecting this is fine. Again you don't want to push a topic you are going to struggle with. Basically just go with it!

Once you have done this you will need to cut the content down. Be careful of doing this because you don't want to get rid of something you might want to use later, but having less to look at and fumble through can make the process much easier to digest.

The meat of the essay (which will later become the body paragraphs) is where all the evidence is addressed and analyzed. If it helps your process, write the meat of the essay in outline form as a placeholder until you have a better sense of the direction you'd like it.

- **A good way to begin this process** is to simply arrange your evidence on paper so that it tells a story – that is, introductory information first, then elaborating details and supporting evidence, then (seemingly) contradictory evidence, and, finally, information that dispels the contradictory evidence and reaffirms the trend. Afterwards, you can write in all the descriptions and connections.
- **It's always a good idea to present evidence that seems to contradict the larger trend.** Addressing and refuting it will make your argument appear stronger.
- **Be aware that the evidence you've gathered may bring you to a different conclusion than you anticipated.** If this happens, adopt the new conclusion as your own and be grateful that your essay has become more logical.

Shortcut When it comes to researching and collecting information quickly it is really effective to search your original topic and gather information that fits together in one document. You can get any kind of source material online, including what will work for book sources and scholarly journals. Don't get to crazy about collecting data, get the bulk from places like news sites, Wikipedia and other websites. You can put it all together later in a way that will be legitimate and original.

BACK

Writing the Paper (Shortcut**)**

Remind to just start somewhere

Spinning rules: three word rule   Write the body paragraphs. These are based on the meat of the essay and should already be largely underway. If you haven't done so already, break up what you've written so far into paragraphs. Though body paragraphs are generally split apart by topic, note that very long paragraphs will have to be broken apart for the readers' sake; look for places to beak that won't disrupt the flow of your writing.

- **Make sure to introduce new topics with "topic sentences"** that let the reader know what you're going to tackle next. A topic sentence is the first sentence of a paragraph, but not every paragraph will necessarily have them (as some topics span multiple paragraphs).

- **The vast majority of each paragraph** should present, elaborate on, and interpret the information you've gathered before coming to a brief extrapolation or conclusion at the end.

Write the conclusion. Now that you have carefully worked through your evidence, write a conclusion that briefly summarizes your findings for the reader and provides a sense of closure. Start by briefly restating the thesis statement, then remind the reader of the points you covered over the course of the paper. Slowly zoom out of the topic as you write, ending on a broad note by emphasizing the larger implication of your findings.

- **The goal of the conclusion**, in very simplified terms, is to answer the question, "So what?" Make sure the reader feels like (s)he's come away with something.
- **It's a good idea to write the conclusion before the introduction** for several reasons. First of all, the conclusion is easier to write when the evidence is still fresh in your mind. On top of that, it's recommended that you use up your most choice language in the conclusion and then reword these ideas less strongly in the introduction, not the other way around; this will leave a more lasting impression on the reader.

Write the introduction. The introduction is, in many respects, the conclusion written in reverse: start by generally introducing the larger topic, then orient the reader in the area you've focused on, and finally, supply the thesis statement. Avoid repeating exact phrases that you already used in the conclusion.

Shortcut When it comes to researching and collecting information quickly it is really effective to search your original topic and gather information that fits together in one document. You can get any kind of source material online, including what will work for book sources and scholarly journals. Don't get to crazy about collecting data, get the bulk from places like news sites, Wikipedia and other websites. You can put it all together later in a way that will be legitimate and original.

BACK

Checking things over (*Shortcut*)

Revise your thesis statement. Now that you have thoroughly examined and processed your information, rewrite your thesis statement to better reflect your findings.

Revise the paper and develop a final draft. Read through the paper at least two or three times. Make sure all of your assertions are backed up by sources, you have transitions between all of your main points, and that you did not leave out any details. Finally, look for any spelling, grammar, punctuation, or word choice errors.

Finishing things up (*Shortcut*)

***

Provide a works cited page. This page includes all of the sources cited in your paper. Write your research paper using APA style/format.

Glossary

***

Abstract

-     **An argumentative research** paper takes a position on a contentious issue and argues for one point of view. The issue should be debatable with a logical counter argument.
-     **An analytical research paper** offers a fresh look at an important issue. The subject may not be controversial, but you must attempt to persuade your audience that your ideas have merit.

Find good sources. Ideally, you should use a variety of sources, including websites, books, academic or professional journals, and interviews with experts. Realistically, however, a lot of your sources will be found online. While using a tertiary source like Wikipedia is not generally accepted in academic papers, Wikipedia articles often have citations linked to source material. Look for **credible**

Spinning is the practice of taking an original text and rewriting it so that it can pass any plagiarism test

.thesis

List of Useful Websites